Argumentative and Aggressive Communication